over tea

over tea
for friends everywhere...

- terri st.cloud

bone sigh books

copyright 2008
all rights reserved
printed in the USA

ISBN: 978-0-9815440-1-4 (pbk)
bone sigh arts
www.bonesigharts.com
www.bonesighbooks.com

the teacup on our cover is a special gift
from our talented potter friend, jenna.
you can find more of her work at
'the labyrinth of life' shop on etsy.com.
thank you jenna for being part of our book!

cover art: yohan
www.bfg-productions.com

book layout / design:
zakk and yo
www.mazuzu.com

contents

contents

there's beauty inside of you.
just waiting for you.
waiting to be held and danced with.

it is to that dance that i dedicate this book.

and to barbara.....
i'll never forget that tea we shared...
this book is yours.

i don't really even know what "inner child" work is, but i think what i do sometimes is probably exactly that. i never quite know how to explain it, because i always sound like a lunatic when i try to share these stories. and that is just one of the beautiful things about friends and tea! you can meet up with them, cozy in to some warm tea and share all the things that make you goofy. and they still love you!

and so, it was over tea that i shared some of my inner child work with a friend. being used to me, she never raised an eyebrow when i launched into my "little terri" story. when i told her that i had asked my inner child for help seeing my beauty, her eyes filled with tears. at that moment, i felt like i could look right down deep inside her. it was then that i knew that she too needed help in finding and holding her beauty. as i got up to leave, i thought to myself, "i really want to give her something that tells her she's beautiful."

and that was the birth of "over tea."

we first offered it in a hand made version, but are so thrilled to offer it in a "real" format here. not to discount the beauty of hand made, but to acknowledge that we can reach a bigger audience this way and terri won't staple her fingers anymore trying to put books together!! (that in itself feels really good!)

the wider audience part is a good thing and a sad thing. why is it so many of us have such trouble seeing our beauty? and then even if we get a glimpse of it...why is it so darn hard to hold on to?! whatever the reasons, i know that reminders and nudges help me with my journey. it is my hope that the following quotes can be reminders and nudges to help you along yours.

if we all understood just how much trouble we're each having seeing our own beauty, maybe we'd help each other more to see. i am amazed at the conversations i end up having with people. seems whenever we're talking about a problem they're having in their life, if we really start getting into it, if we really start trying to go to the core of it all, we end up at the same point always....they don't feel like they matter, they don't feel like they're beautiful. we always seem to land there. how can this be? how is it we don't know our own beauty? maybe we need help from each other. maybe it takes a mirror to see it.

1

my best friend in the whole world and i were trying to figure out what exactly love was. one day he came up with this thought...and it stunned me.

"maybe to love another is to trust them enough to use them as a mirror for the love of one's self." *

you gotta read that a couple of times to let it sink in. (at least i did.) i remember, i actually wrote it down, put it on the counter in front of me while i did dishes and tried to figure it out. there's a lot packed into that one little thought!

someone once came thru that told me they thought that was really self centered. if that's what you're getting out of it, read it again. it's not meant that way. and it so ties in with what i'm trying to say here. find someone you trust, ask your inner child, maybe read this book...

find a mirror...a mirror that really helps you see...and hold the beauty that is yours.

and then dance with that beauty.

*thank you, bob, for allowing me to share your wisdom!

her beauty

i look at her and see beauty,
and yet, she's been told she's not beautiful.
i watch her and see love,
and yet, she's been told she's not lovely.
i want to shout to her,
"you are precious beyond words!"
yet i know she can't hear me.
and so i won't shout.
i will just keep believing in her
and reminding her.
and wait for her to see it,
to hear it,
and to know it
as deeply as i do.

turn your eyes

turn your eyes to yourself.
turn inside and see who you are.
love the little girl inside.
cherish the woman who has emerged
and hold yourself gently.

keeping her strong

she was scared.
to trust seemed an enormous task.
she held onto her friends and let
their trust keep her steady ~
and let their love keep her strong.

birth

she was telling him about giving birth~
"one of the most amazing things about it is
you have to totally trust thru the worst pain.
all you can do is release control and trust."
she stopped and stared at him.
the tears came.
"i guess that's not just during birth,
is it?" she asked, reaching for his hand.

rules

their rules still clutched her tight.
silently strangling her.
it was time to break their grip ~
and their rules.

playing it safe

the fear won't help save what you have -
it will make you lose what you could become.

driving home

the sadness flooded over her.
the tears welled up -
but they didn't spill.
her voice came to her
and stopped them.
"you couldn't be who you are
without this pain."
and she knew that.
she thanked her sorrow,
tucked it away
and drove home.

so easy

she didn't have to figure it out with her head.
all she had to do was listen to her insides
and follow them -
it was so easy it scared her!

underneath

her head ached.
her eyes were red.
and on the upper layer was exhaustion.
underneath, tho,
there was a peace that steadied her.
she felt it,
trusted it,
and leaned towards it.

tackling me

holding nothing back,
she tackles me with real.
with a grin and a tear
she shares her depths.
denying no part of herself,
she encourages me to do the same.
taking my hand,
together,
we face the world.

so much more

yes, there was sadness,
but there was so much more.
belief in herself.
strength that kept growing
and a knowing that she was okay.
and would always be okay.
no one could take that away now.

using it

recognizing her strength,
she decided to use it.

thanks

who do i thank for her?
the stars?
the universe?
she herself?
none of these thanks seem enough for
such a gift as having her in my life.

denise

she speaks of her journey
telling me her truths...
wisdom pours forth and i soak it in.
grace is her countenance,
trust is her being.
i grow just from knowing her.
my soul soars when she is near.

young artist

you can't go wrong, she told the young girl.
if you just feel what's inside of you.
when i look in your eyes, your beauty tumbles out.
let it tumble thru your hands
onto your creations.
don't follow their rules.
make it yours and no one else's.
and believe in that beauty that runs thru you.

making room

he accepted her for all she was.
always making room for her to be.
it was in that room she saw
it wasn't anyone else that needed
to accept her.
it was up to her to do it for herself.

beyond the scars

pushing beyond those old scars,
she kept on.
wanting to be more, she reached out.
the reflection of love
glistened in her tears
and all i could think of
was how precious she was.

a vow to my heart

i will work on the act of listening to you
and my listening abilities will grow.
i will honor those things you
relay to me and act upon them.
when i act upon them, i will know that i am living
my truth and owe no explanations to anyone.
i will believe in your ability to accept all emotions
and will not close down to protect you.
i will direct my energies and my power
to places that will strengthen you,
not deplete you.
i will follow you in the way i wish
the world would follow you.
the child of the universe and the heart
shall meld and we shall dance as one.

tam

i watched her,
admiring her ~
wanting to be like her.
her eyes turned in my direction
reflecting to me my own beauty.
and i came to know it thru
her love.

gratitude

as she thought of her friend,
she recalled hearing that
"gratitude is the heart of prayer."
she smiled, realizing her entire being
was one big prayer at that moment.
and her friend the reason for that
prayer.

her power

she took her power back ~
without permission.

open eyes

her eyes opened to her own beauty
and the ground shook.

souls

she didn't just survive -
she became.

your truth

it is your truth.
your power.
your soul.
guard it with all you have.
don't let anyone's misconceptions steal it.
including your own.

she helped

knowing what i could be,
believing in who i was,
she helped me to become.

for barbara

she touched her friend's arm -
this searching we do,
this trying to grow -
it means so much to me.
but don't ever lose sight of this,
my friend,
in my eyes you are perfect the way
you are.
and it is you that i love.

cleaning

it wasn't just that she had to refocus.
she had to clean her lens.
that dust from the past was
giving her a fuzzy view.
she had some cleaning to do.

for annie

quietly simmering above the fire
her beauty bubbled deep within.
thru confusion and loss it murmured
so quietly she forgot it was there.
but to those of us around her,
it never left our eyes –
and we loved the Light that she was.

my goddess friend

she loves me even tho i don't understand it.
she believes in me when i can't.
i look at her eyes loving me so
and she makes me feel beautiful.

birthing her

she awoke one day
and realized all these steps
she had taken were like labor pains.
the sorrow and grief and confusion
were her contractions.
all leading to the birth of the woman she had become.

galaxies

did she have to drop into it?
maybe it could come swirl her away instead?
either way she had to let go,
didn't she?

me, myself

i commit to me, myself, today.
i vow to listen to and follow and believe
in my goodness.
to recognize my strength
and wield it with the added power of compassion.
to know my heart
and trust it and not turn to outside expectations
to feed it, but rather turn to my own inner guidance
to lead me.
to know that i am the woman i want to be
and work to uncover more of my beauty daily.
and to be gentle with myself when
i slip - loving myself even in the darkness.
to me, myself, i give my love.
and it is from me, myself, my love is returned.

the universe

she talked a lot of trusting the universe –
but what she really meant was trusting herself.
and in some way that she didn't understand yet,
they were the same thing.

tears of recognition

weeping tears of recognition,
she found herself among the ruins
and brought herself back to life.

ground crew

filled with faith and hope,
the ground crew stood by as they
watched her take off.

it was there

it wasn't what she would have chosen to be part of her
but it was there.
she couldn't ignore it any more.
and slowly,
she discovered it's beauty.

energies

sharing their power, they help me find mine.

for mag

it was when she laughed
and smiled
that her beauty grabbed me.
and i loved her.

jennene

making me look without forcing me...
making me question without asking me...
letting me search while keeping me safe...
she leads me home.

giving

maybe when you really love yourself
you can see beyond that self -
and then maybe you never give yourself away.
maybe you just give.

kai's blessing

may you know the fire within you.
may you never doubt your connection to it.
may you learn the balance of holding it close
and giving it freely.
and may you dance with the light that you
shine.

she looks

she looks and sees me.
relief runs thru my veins.
she listens and understands.
i tremble with joy.
she takes my hand and asks me to grow.
i thank god for her.

good friend

the good kind of friend not only
encourages you to grow
and inspires you to grow ~
the good kind of friend makes
you believe you can grow.

new perspective

she had to stop looking at it as
tragic she lost something.
it was time to accept that it would have
been tragic if she never left it.

demons

it's all about facing demons -
and facing demons alone, she said.
it wasn't til she looked them in the eyes
that she saw they were her best friends.

she understood

she closed her eyes,
honoring my pain with her silence ~
and i knew she understood.

fear

her friend's words kept coming back to her...
"your fear is stopping you from being you.
drop it.
it's serving you no purpose.
let it go and allow yourself to be."
she smiled to herself and decided to trust
even more.

trained eyes

their eyes had trained a life time
of looking past her.
and she had gotten her training
from them.
it was time to look at herself,
see the pain,
hold the ache
and love the girl inside.

for lee

her strength poured thru her pain
and i loved her.

doors

her running stopped.
her trusting began.
and slowly the doors creaked open.

melted

the thaw began,
the ice melted
and the world opened up again.

time

it was time to let go of her fear
and embrace her strength.

conviction

it was a total knowing of what she had to do.
every cell in her body knew.
it was conviction.

sisterhood

"i want to give her something to hold,
to have,
to hang on to while she goes thru this,"
she said.
and it was in her very desire
to do so,
she had given the greatest gift of all –
her friendship, her love,
her sisterhood.

moments

there wasn't a moment that went by
that the knowing of what they shared
didn't strengthen her.

beyond sterile

the rules were rigid.
the walls sterile
and touching prohibited,
"but we do it anyway," she said.
for they knew it was those small acts
of love given in secret that saved them.

choices

feeling tiny and helpless
we chose to believe in love –
it was all we had,
it was all we needed.

for kate

plans change.
disappointment happens.
trust speaks.
excitement seeps back in.
and the journey to
'we don't know where' continues...

those that will

they won't always reach back,
she said.
know there are those that will.
love them.
honor the others.
and believe in what
it is you are offering.

if i could

if i could teach you anything –
it would be to
hear your heart,
and to know your beauty
an to believe in your possibilities.

perhaps

perhaps power is letting go of the grip of the past
and standing empty handed facing the
future.

hope

and she had hope

daring

the key was in her daring.

under the trees

it had been a lifetime for others –
and now she wanted to know herself.
sitting under the trees,
she asked herself how she was feeling
and she began to really listen.

terri didn't know she was a writer, didn't know she was an artist, she just plain ol' didn't know a heck of a lot of anything. and then some good ol' fashioned, gut wrenching, heart ripping pain gripped her life, and she started to discover things about herself.

she began her journey inward. when the pain got to be too much for her, she spilled out her feelings on paper. wanting to honor those feelings somehow, she added art to them. it was with that mixing of spilling and honoring that bone sighs were born.

needing to find a way to support herself and her sons, she began peddling her watercolor bone sighs shop to shop. thru an amazing journey of tears, miracles, trust, terror, laughter, squeezing her eyes closed tight, and following her heart, somehow bone sigh arts became a real business.

home made books were offered for awhile among her prints and cards. cumbersome to make and lacking the desired quality, there came a time when the books needed to become "real." grabbing her sons, terri and the guys decided to go into print!

without terri's sons, bone sigh arts/books would never ever have become what it has. funny how the very reason for the business became what made the business successful. those boys are everything to both terri and bone sighs!

josh is the oldest. an old soul musician, born entertainer, and a loveable guy! yo yo is their gentle giant who's turning into the world's best graphic designer! and zakk is the logical one. computer geek and mad inventor with the marshmallow heart.

and! the boys have expanded into beginning their own businesses for themselves! (check out the information page for a listing of their websites!)

it's been quite a journey for them all.

terri's still scratchin' her head wonderin' if she'll ever figure any of it out! probably not....but she'll keep trying anyway!

- info -

terri st.cloud
15809 menk rd
accokeek md 20607
granolastew@gmail.com

bone sigh arts
BoneSighArts.com

bone sigh books
BoneSighBooks.com

Zakk and Yo's business
Mazuzu.com

Yohan's business
BFG-Productions.com

Josh's business
Poodleman.com